# Praying the Scriptures

**STUDY GUIDE**

Catherine Upchurch
Clifford M. Yeary

## LITTLE ROCK SCRIPTURE STUDY

*A ministry of the Diocese of Little Rock
in partnership with Liturgical Press*

## DIOCESE OF LITTLE ROCK

2500 North Tyler Street • P.O. Box 7565 • Little Rock, Arkansas 72217 • (501) 664-0340 Fax (501) 664-6304

Dear Friends in Christ,

Sacred Scripture is a wealth of inspired wisdom expressing Christian truths which challenge us to deepen our relationship with God. Although the Bible can be intimidating, it is important that we study God's word in the Scriptures, because it is the basis of our faith and offers us the thoughts and experiences of Christians past and present. It is God speaking to us through the insights of Church fathers and later saints.

I am pleased to present this study guide from Little Rock Scripture Study to serve as an aid for reflection and contemplation in your reading of Scripture. At the same time, the guide will give you insight into how to apply what you have read to your life today.

I encourage you to read Sacred Scripture slowly and reflectively so that it can penetrate your heart and mind. It is my hope that the Word of God will empower you as Christians to live a life worthy of your call as a child of God and a member of the body of Christ.

Sincerely in Christ,

✝ Anthony B. Taylor
Bishop of Little Rock

# Sacred Scripture

"The Church has always venerated the divine Scriptures just as she venerates the body of the Lord, since from the table of both the word of God and of the body of Christ she unceasingly receives and offers to the faithful the bread of life, especially in the sacred liturgy. She has always regarded the Scriptures together with sacred tradition as the supreme rule of faith, and will ever do so. For, inspired by God and committed once and for all to writing, they impart the word of God Himself without change, and make the voice of the Holy Spirit resound in the words of the prophets and apostles. Therefore, like the Christian religion itself, all the preaching of the Church must be nourished and ruled by sacred Scripture. For in the sacred books, the Father who is in heaven meets His children with great love and speaks with them; and the force and power in the word of God is so great that it remains the support and energy of the Church, the strength of faith for her sons, the food of the soul, the pure and perennial source of spiritual life."

Vatican II, Dogmatic Constitution on Divine Revelation, no. 21.

## INTERPRETATION OF SACRED SCRIPTURE

"Since God speaks in sacred Scripture through men in human fashion, the interpreter of sacred Scripture, in order to see clearly what God wanted to communicate to us, should carefully investigate what meaning the sacred writers really intended, and what God wanted to manifest by means of their words.

"Those who search out the intention of the sacred writers must, among other things, have regard for 'literary forms.' For truth is proposed and expressed in a variety of ways, depending on whether a text is history of one kind or another, or whether its form is that of prophecy, poetry, or some other type of speech. The interpreter must investigate what meaning the sacred writer intended to express and actually expressed in particular circumstances as he used contemporary literary forms in accordance with the situation of his own time and culture. For the correct understanding of what the sacred author wanted to assert, due

attention must be paid to the customary and characteristic styles of perceiving, speaking, and narrating which prevailed at the time of the sacred writer, and to the customs men normally followed in that period in their everyday dealings with one another."
Vatican II, Dogmatic Constitution on Divine Revelation, no. 12.

# *Instructions*

## MATERIALS FOR THE STUDY

**This Study Guide:** Praying the Scriptures

**Bible:** The New American Bible with Revised New Testament or The New Jerusalem Bible is recommended. Paraphrased editions are discouraged as they offer little if any help when facing difficult textual questions. Choose a Bible you feel free to write in or underline.

**Commentary:** *Praying the Scriptures* by Demetrius Dumm, O.S.B. (Liturgical Press) is used with this study. The assigned pages are found at the beginning of each lesson.

## ADDITIONAL MATERIALS

**Bible Dictionary:** *The Dictionary of the Bible* by John L. McKenzie (Simon & Schuster) is highly recommended as a reference.

**Notebook:** A notebook may be used for lecture notes and your personal reflections.

## WEEKLY LESSONS

Lesson 1—Introduction, Chapter 1: I will declare all your wondrous deeds. (Ps 9:2)
Lesson 2—Chapter 2: Say to God, "How awesome your deeds!" (Ps 66:3)
Lesson 3—Chapter 3: Father, I thank you for hearing me. (John 11:41)
Lesson 4—Chapter 4: The bread that I will give is my flesh for the life of the world. (John 6:51)

Lesson 5—Chapter 5: Pray without ceasing. (1 Thess 5:17)
Lesson 6—Chapter 6: [L]et us continually offer a sacrifice of
praise to God. (Heb 13:15); Conclusion.


## YOUR DAILY PERSONAL STUDY

The first step is prayer. Open your heart and mind to God.
Reading Scripture is an opportunity to listen to God who
loves you. Pray that the same Holy Spirit who guided the
formation of Scripture will inspire you to correctly understand what you read and empower you to make what you
read a part of your life.

The next step is commitment. Daily spiritual food is as
necessary as food for the body. This study is divided into
daily units. Schedule a regular time and place for your study,
as free from distractions as possible. Allow about twenty
minutes a day. Make it a daily appointment with God.

As you begin each lesson read the indicated pages of the
commentary and the appropriate Scripture passage where
indicated. This preparation will give you an overview of the
entire lesson and help you to appreciate the context of indi-
vidual passages.

As you reflect on Scripture, ask yourself these four questions:

1. *What does the Scripture passage say?*
   Read the passage slowly and reflectively. Use your imagi-
   nation to picture the scene or enter into it.

2. *What does the Scripture passage mean?*
   Read the footnotes and the commentary to help you understand what the sacred writers intended and what God
   wanted to communicate by means of their words.

3. *What does the Scripture passage mean to me?*
   Meditate on the passage. God's Word is living and power-
   ful. What is God saying to you today? How does the Scripture passage apply to your life today?

4. *What am I going to do about it?*
   Try to discover how God may be challenging you in this passage. An encounter with God contains a challenge to know God's will and follow it more closely in daily life.

## THE QUESTIONS ASSIGNED FOR EACH DAY

Read the questions and references for each day. The questions are designed to help you listen to God's Word and to prepare you for the weekly small-group discussion.

Some of the questions can be answered briefly and objectively by referring to the Bible references and the commentary *(What does the passage say?)*. Some will lead you to a better understanding of how the Scriptures apply to the Church, sacraments, and society *(What does the passage mean?)*. Some questions will invite you to consider how God's Word challenges or supports you in your relationships with God and others *(What does the passage mean to me?)*. Finally, the questions will lead you to examine your actions in light of Scripture *(What am I going to do about it?)*.

Write your responses in this study guide or in a notebook to help you clarify and organize your thoughts and feelings.

## THE WEEKLY SMALL-GROUP MEETING

The weekly small-group sharing is the heart of the Little Rock Scripture Study Program. Participants gather in small groups to share the results of praying, reading, and reflecting on Scripture and on the assigned questions. The goal of the discussion is for group members to be strengthened and nourished individually and as a community through sharing how God's Word speaks to them and affects their daily lives. The daily study questions will guide the discussion; it is not necessary to discuss all the questions.

All members share the responsibility of creating an atmosphere of loving support and trust in the group by respecting the opinions and experiences of others, and by affirming and encouraging one another. The simple shared prayer which begins and ends each small group meeting also helps create the open and trusting environment in which group members can share their faith deeply and grow in the study of God's Word.

A distinctive feature of this program is its emphasis on and trust in God's presence working in and through each member. Sharing responses to God's presence in the Word and in others can bring about remarkable growth and transformation.

## THE WRAP-UP LECTURE

The lecture is designed to develop and clarify the themes of the lesson. It is not intended to form the basis for the group discussion. For this reason the lecture is always held at the end of the meeting. If several small groups meet at one time, the large group will gather together in a central location to listen to the lecture.

Lectures may be given by a local speaker. They are also available in audio form on CD, and in visual form on DVD.

# LESSON 1

*Praying the Scriptures,* pages vii–xi, 1–24

**Day 1**

1.  How important to your life is having a sense of meaning?

2.  How has your reading the *words* of Scripture led you to consider what God has actually *done* in your life and in the lives of others?

3.  a) What is the simple key to fruitful reading of the Scriptures according to the commentary? (See p. 3.)
    b) What is the key event in the Old Testament? And in the New Testament?

**Day 2**

4.  In reading the story of creation (Gen 1-4), what are some of the themes that show a connection to the Exodus experience? (Skim Exod 1-20.)

5.  Describe a personal experience with creation that led you to a new appreciation of God's ongoing creative activity (Ps 65). (See also Ps 19:2; 29; 104; 135:5-7; Isa 45:18; Rom 1:20.)

6.  If God has commanded humans to "fill the earth and subdue it" (Gen 1:28), and to have "dominion" over it, why can't we do whatever we will to it? (See Gen 1:31.)

## Day 3

7. How do the elements in the celebration of Passover (Exod 12:7-8, 11, 14) help every generation make the events of the Exodus their own? (See Exod 12:24-27.)

8. Israel's salvation begins with a cry for help (Exod 1:13-14; 2:23b-25) which leads to God's generous response (Exod 3:7-8).

   a) How is this pattern repeated in salvation history (Ps 40)? (See samples: Isa 19:20; 30:19; Neh 9:26-27; Heb 5:7; Rev 6:9-10; 21:3-5.)

   b) How is this pattern repeated in your life? (See Ps 34:5-11, 18-19.)

9. Who has been a "Moses" in our society? In our Church? In your life?

## Day 4

10. What does God pledge and ask for in the covenant on Sinai (Exod 19:2-8)? (See Deut 4:32-40; 1 Pet 2:9.)

11. a) What is the significance of God giving the law to former slaves only after setting them free from oppression in Egypt? (See Ps 40; 135:8-14.)

    b) The call to obey God's law is often coupled with a remembrance of God's goodness (Deut 32:7-14). How has your own remembrance of God's goodness in your life equipped you to be faithful?

12. Given our call to live in God's freedom, where do the commandments most challenge our culture (Exod 20:1-17)?

**Day 5**

13. The earliest proclamations of the good news show the intimate link between suffering and resurrection (Mark 16:6-7; Acts 2:22-24, 36; 1 Cor 1:18; 15:3-5).

    How does this message continue to challenge us to reevaluate the meaning of success and failure? (See Matt 5:1-12; Luke 6:20-26; 1 Cor 7:29-31; 2 Cor 8:9.)

14. In what ways does the passion and resurrection of Jesus give fuller meaning to creation and the Exodus? (See Luke 9:28-36; Rom 8:18-22.)

15. Recall a time when your own prayer was filled with praise. How might such a moment help you to appreciate what is meant by the victory of Jesus, the "Lamb that was slain" (Rev 5:11-14)?

**Day 6**

16. Throughout Scripture, God's activity in the world is experienced as loving kindness / mercy *(hesed)* and faithfulness *(emeth)*. (See Exod 34:6-9; Deut 7:9; Ps 30:6; 86:4-5, 15; 89; Lam 3:22-23.) How has our Church been a strong sign of God's mercy and faithfulness?

17. Where have you seen evidence of right, goodness, and humility (Micah 6:8) in world, national, or local events?

18. What events of this day lead you to praise and thank God?

# LESSON 2

*Praying the Scriptures,* pages 25–52

## Day 1

1.  What insight from the previous lesson (personal study, faith sharing, wrap-up lecture) gave you a new perspective for your prayer?

2.  What can you do to deepen your experience of the words of Scripture and truly participate in God's saving deeds described there (Eph 1:18-20)? (See Deut 5:2-3; Rom 6:4; 12:2; Col 2:13.)

3.  How can events and relationships in one's life highlight the need for conversion from selfishness? (See Luke 12:16-21; 1 Cor 10:24; Phil 2:3.) Give an example.

## Day 2

4.  In what ways does the story of the woman who anointed Jesus (Mark 14:3-9) foreshadow Jesus' own action for us in his passion and death (Mark 15:21-41)?

5.  a) How can being "justified by God's grace" (Rom 3:24) create a positive attitude toward life? (See Rom 5:1; 8:28-37.)

    b) How is believing creeds or statements of faith different from *having* faith?

6.  What is it about David's faith that is more pleasing to God than Saul's faith? (See 1 Sam 15:11; 16:7; 2 Sam 7:18-29; 22:1-4, 21-31.)

**Day 3**

7. Identify the elements in the account of Jesus' baptism (Mark 1:9-13) that indicate God is doing something new in the world. (See Gen 1:1-2; Isa 63:19–64:1.)

8. How does our own baptism invite us to experience God's love as Jesus did (Gal 4:4-7)? (See Rom 9:25-26; Eph 4:21-24; Col 3:12-14.)

9. What are some of the obstacles that interfere with hearing and believing that the Father calls each of us beloved sons and daughters (Mark 1:11)? (See 1 John 2:15-17; 3:1-3.)

**Day 4**

10. What sources of security are promoted by our culture? Do these things lead to a greater sense of peace in the lives of individuals and communities?

11. What type of security is promoted throughout the Bible (1 John 1:1-3)? (See Ps 46; John 10:27-28; 15:15; 1 Pet 1:3-5.)

12. Select one of the following Psalms to pray for several days as you meditate on your source of security in everyday life: Psalms 23; 27; 33; 62; 130. How did the words of the psalmist help you still yourself and grow in a sense of true security before God?

**Day 5**

13. Compose a list of those things God has done for you that you might include in a personal psalm reminding you to trust God when times are difficult. (See these examples from Israel's life: Ps 65:6-14; 68:8-11; 105; 136.)

14. a) Describe the differences between lamenting (Ps 13:1-2) and complaining (Exod 16:1-3; 17:1-7).

    b) How is your understanding of Jesus' passion (Matt 27:45-50; Mark 15:34) transformed once you become familiar with all of Psalm 22 as Jesus would have known it?

15. How does an appreciation of Jesus' lament on the cross suggest a way for us to pray for ourselves and others in times of despair?

**Day 6**

16. Israel often expressed its yearning for God as a "thirst" (Ps 143:5-8). (See Ps 42:1-3; 63:1; Isa 55:1.) What are some other images to express your yearning for God?

17. In what ways have you become aware of God accompanying you as you move from the faith of childhood to a more mature faith? (See 1 Cor 13:11; Heb 5:13-14.)

18. Where in your daily life do you have opportunities to set people free? (See Ps 146:5-9; Isa 58:6; Luke 4:18-19.)

# LESSON 3

*Praying the Scriptures,* pages 53–80

## Day 1

1.  What events of the last week might lead you to give thanks to God? To lament? Were you ever tempted to complain?

2.  How do some of the various Scripture passages that emphasize the humanness of Jesus also demonstrate the depth of God's love for us? (See Luke 22:42-44; John 11:35; 15:13; Heb 2:17-18; 4:15-16; 5:7-10.)

3.  How does knowing that Jesus had to struggle with possible consequences of his mission affect the way you pray about your own future (Luke 22:42; Heb 4:15)?

## Day 2

4.  How might the harsh words of Jesus about division (Matt 10:34) be reconciled with the other passages that show Jesus did not want his cause associated with violence (Matt 26:52)? (See Matt 5:9; John 14:27; Rom 12:17-18; 2 Cor 13:11.)

5.  a) Identify if you can an instance in your life when it was necessary to trust someone and your trust was rewarded.

    b) What major events in the history of Israel and Judah demonstrate the necessity for the people to live in trust in their relationship to God? (See 2 Kgs 17:1-6; 24:10-14; 1 Macc 1:10-24.)

6.  How would it change your life to pray wholeheartedly with the Psalms, "Be still," (Ps 37:1-7; 131) and "wait for the Lord" (Ps 27:11-14; 37:7-9; 130)?

**Day 3**

7. How can praying Scripture that expresses emotion other than what we are actually feeling help free us from self-centeredness? (Consider the variety of emotions found in the Psalms.)

8. What is the goal of persevering in prayer according to Luke 11:9-13? What is the goal in the other two Synoptic accounts? (See Mark 11:22-24; Matt 7:7-11.)

9. Jesus suggests that the ultimate goal of persevering in prayer is to receive the gift of the Holy Spirit (Luke 11:1-13). How is the Spirit's guidance seen in Jesus' own prayer in the Garden of Gethsemane (Luke 22:39-46)? (See Rom 8:26.)

**Day 4**

10. Jesus proclaims, "The kingdom of heaven is at hand" (Matt 4:17).

    a) What would the first hearers of Jesus' proclamation have understood or expected?

    b) What do we usually think of?

    c) What was Jesus intending to convey?

11. Why would the evangelists place their transfiguration accounts immediately after a statement such as this: "There are some standing here who will not taste death until they see that the kingdom of God has come in power" (Mark 9:1)? (See Matt 17:1-8; Mark 9:2-8; Luke 9:28-36.)

12. a) What is *Jesus* doing both at his baptism and at the Transfiguration that only Luke identifies (Luke 3:21-22)?

    b) How is this information important for our own relationship with God?

**Day 5**

13. How do the associations with clouds and tents found in the following verses also add to our understanding of Jesus' transfiguration? (See Gen 18:1-6; Exod 33:7-10; 2 Chron 5:13-14; Ps 15.)

14. What does the transfiguration mean for Jesus and his understanding of his mission (Matt 17:9-13)? What does it mean for Peter and the disciples (Matt 17:2-8)?

15. How might the pleas for forgiveness found in three Psalms attributed to David affect his reputation as a model and example for Israel? (See Ps 25:1-7; 38:1-3; 51.)

**Day 6**

16. What is the significance of Pilate's question in John 18:33 and Jesus' response to him in verse 34? Why is Pilate's personal position on the matter important to Jesus?

17. According to the Gospel of John (14:16-17; 15:26; 16:7-13), what is the role of the Holy Spirit in helping us to see and respond to the truth that is in Jesus?

18. When has following Jesus required you to trust God when there seemed to be no external evidence of God's love and care?

# LESSON 4

*Praying the Scriptures,* pages 81–110

## Day 1

1. What did you learn in the last lesson about Jesus as a model of prayer that encourages you to pray with more confidence?

2. What is the significance of speaking of both the real presence and symbolic presence of Christ in the Eucharist?

3. How would you describe the difference between the joy of deliverance and being able to trust the deliverer (Num 14:1-4; Ps 95:6-9; 114:1-4)? Have you had any experience that can help you understand this difference in a personal way?

## Day 2

4. Does it surprise you to know that the Hebrew slaves adapted an existing ritual to commemorate their exodus from Egypt (Exod 12:1-20)? What rituals from your daily life could become signs of God's continuing presence if you consciously chose to make the connection?

5. a) How can our rituals when celebrating the Liturgy of the Word invite us to deeper participation in the mission of Jesus in the world?

   b) How does the Liturgy of the Eucharist insure that every assembly can participate in the one-time event of Jesus' passion, death, and resurrection even now?

6. How has your participation in the celebration of Eucharist helped to make real to you the saving events of Christ?

**Day 3**

7. What is Jesus modeling for his followers when he proclaims that the bread and wine of the Last Supper are his own body and blood (Phil 2:4-8)? (See Matt 26:26-28; Mark 14:22-24; Luke 17:19-20.)

8. Like ancient Israel (Deut 5:15; 15:15; 16:12; 24:17-22), the Church remembers God's deeds of mercy in story and ritual. How does the "anamnesis" following the consecration move us beyond simply recalling the past to living differently because of it?

9. Why is our "Amen" one of the most important words we express in worship? (See 1 Chron 16:34-36; Rom 16:25-27; 2 Cor 1:18-20.)

**Day 4**

10. a) What associations do you have with the word "Father" that either enhance or interfere with praying the Lord's Prayer?

    b) What is intended in the use of "Our Father" when Jesus taught his disciples how to pray and invited them to address God in this way? (See Matt 6:9-13; Luke 11:2-4; Jas 1:17.)

    c) What does Jesus' relationship with his heavenly Father teach human fathers about their relationship with their children?

11. How do the three petitions in the Lord's Prayer that concern God help you in your overall relationship with God and your participation in the building of the kingdom?

12. What forms of daily nourishment come to mind when praying "give us today our daily bread" (Matt 6:11)? (See Isa 25:6-8; 55:2; John 6:48-51, 57-58.)

**Day 5**

13. When has an experience of offering forgiveness to another person helped you to experience God's mercy in your own life (Matt 6:12, 14-15; 7:1-2)? (See Luke 17:3-4; Eph 4:32.)

14. In what ways can our believing communities move beyond ritual celebration of the Eucharist to living its effects? Can you think of illustrations of this kind of "eucharistic" lifestyle within your own parish? (See John 6:31-35, 40, 47-58; Acts 2:42-47; 1 Cor 11:27-28.)

15. Do you think your parish community adequately expresses both the suffering and the glory of Jesus in its celebration of the Eucharist (Heb 12:1-2)? (See John 17:1-5; Heb 2:9.)

**Day 6**

16. What moments of this life provide for you a foretaste of eternal life? (See Eph 2:4-7; 1 Pet 5:10.)

17. a) What is God creating in your life that leads you to echo the praise found in Revelation 4:11?

    b) How does your celebration of the Eucharist help you to praise God in your daily life?

18. What aspects of the Mass fill you with hope for the realization of God's kingdom (Rev 21:1-7)?

# LESSON 5

*Praying the Scriptures,* pages 111–40

## Day 1

1. What do you remember from last week that continues to help you pray the Lord's Prayer with greater confidence or understanding, or connect more personally with the celebration of the Eucharist?

2. How is attentiveness to the Lord (Deut 6:4-5; Matt 22:37-38) likely to make the second great commandment that much easier to fulfill? (See Lev 19:18; Matt 22:39.)

3. How might such thoughts as Paul urges in Phil 4:8 be considered attentiveness to the Lord? How might they also be part of one's unceasing prayer?

## Day 2

4. a) How does what Paul claims of our relationship to God through the Spirit (Rom 8:9-17) echo Jesus' own experience at his baptism? (See Mark 1:11.)

   b) What are some ways the Spirit can assist our prayers (Rom 8:26-27)? (See Rom 15:30; 1 Cor 14:13-15; Eph 6:18; Phil 1:18-19.)

5. How does knowing that New Testament writers refer to all the baptized as "saints" influence how you regard your brothers and sisters in Christ in your own worshiping community? (See Acts 9:32, 41; 2 Cor 1:1; Eph 1:1; Phil 1:1; Jude 1:3.)

6. a) According to James, what should one who is ill in a Christian community do (Jas 5:14-16)? How can we encourage someone who is very sick to expect some kind of healing from prayer and anointing?

   b) When has your prayerful preparation for any sacrament had a noticeable affect on your appreciation of the sacrament?

**Day 3**

7.  How would you describe the response to himself that Jesus seems to be looking for in the Gospels? Is it enough to know a "right" answer? (See Matt 16:13-15; Mark 8:27-29; Luke 9:18-20; 18:18-23; John 1:35-39.)

8.  What is the possible significance between the time of day mentioned in John 1:39 and the time mentioned in Genesis 3:8?

9.  Prayerfully read the following Scripture passages that speak of a yearning, a hunger, or a thirst for God (Ps 42:2-3; 63:2; 84:3; 119:81, 123-125; 130:5; Isa 26:9; Sir 24:1-20; Matt 5:6). What do you think is actually being sought from God in such prayers?

**Day 4**

10. What stages of development in personal faith do you see in the man who was born blind (John 9:1-41)?

11. How do the Pharisees of John 9 progressively show their blindness?

12. a) How can we distinguish between the wisdom and knowledge that comes from learning and study, and that which comes from personal faith? (See Jer 8:9; 1 Cor 1:20-25; 3:18-20; 2 Cor 1:12; Jas 1:5; 3:13; 1 Tim 6:20.)

    b) How does the wisdom prayed for in Ephesians 1:15-17 differ from the wisdom gained through study and learning?

**Day 5**

13. a) What parts of the account of Jesus' raising of Lazarus from the dead (John 11:1-44) most clearly show that Jesus, and therefore God, can be moved by human suffering?

    b) How do these additional examples of Jesus' compassion encourage you to present your needs and frailties to God? (See Exod 3:7-8; Isa 63:8-9; Matt 11:28-30; 15:32; Luke 7:11-14; Heb 4:15.)

14. How do Jesus' responses to Martha and Mary encourage them to place their faith in his care for them in the present, rather than just for what he will do at the end of time (John 11:20-27, 32-40.)

15. Besides the different settings and situations, what are the similarities and differences in how Jesus, Mary, and Martha relate to each other in the accounts found in Luke 10:38-42 and John 11:1-44?

**Day 6**

16. John 14:9 states, "Whoever has seen me has seen the Father." How does Jesus go on to describe the mystical union between himself, the Father, and believers? (See John 14:23.) How is this union described in Eph 5:25-32?

17. a) How is the truth of God's infinite love for us shown in the personal call of Jesus to his believers? (See John 1:45-49; 4:39-42; 10:14-16.)

    b) How does the importance of hearing Jesus' voice (John 10:14-16) give added significance to
    —Mary and Martha's brother in the tomb? (See John 11:43.)
    —Mary Magdalen at the empty tomb? (See John 20:13-16.)

18. Is it necessary to actually see Jesus in order to have the special relationship to Jesus described in the Gospel of John? (See John 20:28-29.)

# LESSON 6

*Praying the Scriptures,* pages 141–82

## Day 1

1.  What ideas were shared in last week's discussion or wrap-up lecture that were particularly helpful to you?

    *Note: This week's lesson will allow you to read the final chapter of the commentary and choose to "pray with" one or more biblical characters each day. The Study Guide will supply one or two questions per day simply as a way of helping you focus your personal prayer after reading a section of the final chapter. When the small group members meet together, you may wish to speak about your prayer experiences or insights.*

    *This is an opportunity to actually enter into prayer itself, and to reflect on the experience. Plan to set aside a full twenty minutes or so each day to pray, and reflect on the questions below.*

2.  Reflect on the words of trusting response given by Mary (Luke 1:38), Abraham (Gen 22:1), Isaiah (Isa 6:8), and others (Exod 3:4; Acts 9:10). What occasions your own prayer of trust in God's goodness and availability for God's direction? Do the words of availability of these faithful people challenge you?

## Day 2

3.  What is it about Mary that most appeals to you as you continue to grow in faith? (See Luke 1:46-55; 2:51; John 19:25-27.)

4.  What role does the rosary play in your on-going journey with God? How can the Mysteries lead you to a greater appreciation for the saving events in the life of Jesus?

**Day 3**

5.  Consider the life of Abraham (Genesis) or Moses (Exodus and Numbers). In your prayer ask God to give you some of the spirit found in either of these men who helped to shape the faith of Israel and the Church. Whose spirit would be of most benefit to you? Why?

6.  What impresses you about the songs of Moses (Exod 15:1-18) and of Miriam (Exod 15:20-21)? What role does joy play in your own prayer life?

**Day 4**

7.  What can the remaining Old Testament characters outlined in the commentary (pp. 156—61) model for you about prayer? Consider King David, King Solomon, Tobit, Judith, and Job.

8.  Which of the passages from the prophets most clearly expresses your own experience and commitment to the covenant God makes with us? Why? (See Isa 9:5; 12:2-6; Jer 8:23–9:3; 17:14-18; Ezek 37:11-14; Dan 9:4-6, 17-19; Joel 2:15-17.)

**Day 5**

9.  Select a passage from one of the Gospels that can help you meditate on the power of prayer. What passage did you read and reflect on? Why?

10. The commentary provides insights into prayer from the writings of St. Paul. Use the words of any of Paul's greetings (e.g., Gal 1:2-5; 1 Cor 1:4-8; Phil 1:3-6; Eph 1:15-19) as you pray for your family and friends. How does the tone of gratitude begin to permeate the way you then pray for their needs and concerns?

**Day 6**

11. From among the words of Paul found in Rom 8:12-17, 26-27; Eph 6:18-20; and 1 Tim 1:12-13, what most shapes your own prayer at this time in your life?

12. What does it mean to you to "pray without ceasing" (1 Thess 5:17)? How has this study helped to encourage you in this regard?

# NOTES